THE ITALIAN FOOD LOVER'S BOOK OF DAYS

MENU

Piroscalo REGINA MARGHERITA

19 MAGGIO 1900

PRANZO

Riso con purè di piselli

Antipasto assortito

Costolettine alla Ville-roi

Manzo alla Godard

Carciofi alla Spagnuola

Pernici arrosto

INSALATA

TORTA CONVERSAZIONE

Vino Corvo

Formaggio Frutta

Caffè

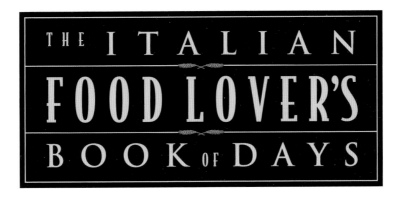

THE ITALIAN FOOD LOVER'S BOOK OF DAYS

TEN SPEED PRESS
BERKELEY, CALIFORNIA

A Kirsty Melville book

Ten Speed Press
P.O. Box 7123
Berkeley, CA 94707

Front cover image copyright Museo Nazionale delle Paste
Alimentari, Rome
Back cover image courtesy Carlo Alberto Bertozzi
See page 119 for additional acknowledgments

Printed in Korea
Design: Aufuldish & Warinner
Picture research: Jan Hughes, U.S.; Studio Ikona, Rome, Italy
Text research: Julia Cain

ISBN 0-89815-735-8

*You may have the universe if
I may have Italy.*

−Giuseppe Verdi

January

1	
New Year's Day	
1449 b. Lorenzo de Medici, Florentine ruler and arts patron	

2	
A.D. 18 d. Ovid, Roman poet	

3

4

5

6

Epiphany (Italy)

7

A man who has not been to Italy is always conscious of his inferiority.

Samuel Johnson, 1776

ODE TO WINE

Bacchus, Bacchus, shout with glee,
Keep on stowing the wine inside;
Then we'll wreck the place noisily.
Drink up, you, and get pie-eyed.
Can't dance any more, I'm fried.
Everybody cry hail, hurray!

> From "Orfeo: Sacrifice of the Bacchantes in Honor of Bacchus,"
> Angelo Poliziano, tutor to the sons of Lorenzo de Medici,
> fifteenth century

Italia! Oh Italia! thou who hast
The fatal gift of beauty

> Byron, Childe Harold, 1818

Opposite: Apollo, Bacco e Sileno al convito nuziale,
Giulio Romano (1499–1546). Palazzo del Te', Mantova (detail)

8

9

1324 d. Marco Polo, explorer

10

11

12

13

New Year's Day—Julian calendar

14

ITALIAN COOKING

~ *"Italian" cooking is a concept of foreigners—to Italians, there is Florentine cooking, Venetian cooking, the cooking of Genoa, Rome, Naples, Sicily, Lombardy and the Adriatic coast. Not only have the provinces retained their own traditions of cookery, but many of their products remain localized.* ~

Elizabeth David, Italian Food

THE BIRTH OF RAVIOLI

~ *Genoa is celebrated for having invented ravioli, which then spread throughout Italy.* ~

Ada Boni, Italian Regional Cooking

Above: Veduta di Genova nel 1481. Museo Navale di Pegli, Genova (detail)

Opposite: Pianta panoramica di Genova, Danti Ignazio (1536–1586). Galleria delle Carte Geografiche Vaticano

15

16

17

18

19

20

21

*Piacenza, Reggio, and
Parma all claim to be the
home of Parmesan cheese—
thus the trade name
Parmigiano-reggiano, which
satisfies two of those claims.*

Ada Boni, Italian Regional Cooking

⌐ *A sharp cheese-grater is an essential tool in any
kitchen where Parmesan cheese is used. In Italy, they are
shaped like round boxes—the grater is the lid, and the
grated cheese falls inside the box.* ⌐
Elizabeth David, Italian Food

TARTUFI CON FORMAGGIO

TRUFFLES AND CHEESE

❦ Wash, brush, and clean eight ounces of truffles,
and slice them. Meanwhile fry four ounces of butter
with one or two tablespoonfuls of pure olive oil; put
in the sliced truffles with four ounces of good Swiss
cheese cut in fine slices. Mix well together over a
brisk fire for ten minutes. Season with pepper and
salt, and serve very hot with croutons.

Janet Ross, Leaves from Our Tuscan Kitchen

The moving line of hills is reflected in the grassy stream; wherein the vintage swells, and the trembling tendrils of the absent vine yet sway.

Ausonius, Mosella

22

A.D. 304 d. St. Vincent of Saragossa, patron of wine industry (Feast Day)

23

24

25

26

Australia Day (Australia)

27

28

LA STRADA MIA (MY STREET)

If a disturbing thought crosses my mind,
I stop for a drink and I console myself with wine:
then I go happily on my way
with destiny in my hand.

Trilussa (Carlo Alberto Salustri), twentieth century

VINO CALDO

HOT WINE

❧ Put into the saucepan one pint of red or white wine, the first preferred. Add two heaping table-spoons of sugar, a piece of rind of lemon or orange, and a small stick of cinnamon. Put it onto the fire and stir until the sugar is dissolved. When the wine boils, strain it through some cheese-cloth and pour it into glasses, and serve hot.

Antonia Isola, Simple Italian Cookery

February

29	
30	
31	
1	
2	
3	
4	

THE CATS OF SANTA ANNA

Housewife, I warn you, keep your wits and eye
    upon the cook-pot boiling at the hearth;
Look! Run! A cat is dragging the veal steak by!
    I'll make another try,
Because a complete sonnet is of no avail
Unless it resembles the cats in having a tail.

    Torquato Tasso, sixteenth century

SNAILS AND FENNEL

    Edible land snails in Istria and elsewhere in Europe feed on wild fennel, and their flesh takes on a bit of its flavor. Several regional dishes, including *insalata di lumache e finocchio*, or snail and fennel salad, take advantage of this fact, and combine snails with fennel.

    Lidia Bastianich and Jay Jacobs,
    La Cucina di Lidia

GREEN MUSHROOMS?

    In Istria, folk wisdom holds that wild mushrooms should be cooked with a piece of brass: if the brass turns green, the mushrooms are thought to be poisonous.

    Lidia Bastianich and Jay Jacobs,
    La Cucina di Lidia

Opposite: La Cuoca, Bernardo Strozzi (1581–1644).
Palazzo Rosso, Genova (detail)

5

1887 Verdi's Othello first produced

6

7

8

9

1893 Verdi's Falstaff first produced

10

11

Pasta alla Norma

12 oz spaghetti
1 lb canned Italian tomatoes
6 tbsp extra virgin olive oil
3 medium eggplants
1 garlic clove
1 tbsp minced basil
1 tbsp grated ricotta salata
oil for frying
salt and pepper

❊ Wash and cut the eggplant lengthwise into thin slices, salt them and put them under a weight for about an hour to squeeze out their water. Crush the garlic and brown it in a saucepan with the olive oil. Add the tomatoes and basil to the saucepan. Salt and pepper to taste and continue cooking for 20 minutes. Dry the slices of eggplant and fry them in abundant oil, then drain them on paper towels. Cook the spaghetti al dente, drain and mix it in a serving bowl with the grated ricotta salata cheese. Add the tomato sauce and fried eggplant slices, mix thoroughly and serve immediately.

Oretta Zanini de Vita, Italy, Italy

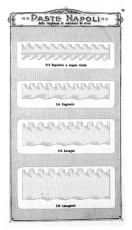

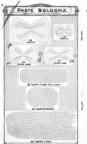

Fettuccine alla Papalina

14 oz egg noodles
4 oz prosciutto, cut in small strips
1 small scallion, chopped
8 oz fresh peas, shelled
3 eggs
3 heaping tbsp grated Parmesan
2 tbsp heavy cream
3 oz butter
salt and pepper

❧ Sauté the scallion and prosciutto in a tablespoon of the butter, add the peas, salt lightly and add a few tablespoons of hot water. Cook, covered. Meanwhile, in a blender, process together the eggs, 2 tablespoons Parmesan and the cream. Cook the pasta al dente. Melt the remaining butter in a large pan, add the egg mixture and let the eggs just begin to cook, stirring quickly with a wire whisk. Add the peas and the pasta, well drained. Mix quickly next to the flame, turn out onto a platter, and sprinkle with the remaining Parmesan.

Oretta Zanini de Vita, Italy, Italy

> *He who bears chives on his breath*
> *Is safe from being kissed to death.*
>
> Marcus Valerius Martialis, c. A.D. 100

12

13

14

Valentine's Day

15

16

17

18

1564 d. Michelangelo Buonarotti, sculptor, painter, architect, and poet

If only but one day I do not meet you,
There is no place where I can find delight;
But if I see you, then I want to eat you,
For one who starves, must sate his appetite.
Michelangelo, Complete Poems of Michelangelo
Translated by Joseph Tusiani

She burns me, binds me, tastes like a lump of sugar.
Michelangelo, line written on the back of a letter dated
24 December, 1507

19

20

21

22

ancient Roman family reunion day

23

24

25

ZABAGLIONE

TRADITIONAL PUDDING

6 egg yolks
6 tablespoons sugar
¾ cup Marsala wine

❀ Beat together all ingredients until thoroughly blended. Put in top of a double boiler over boiling water, and continue to beat until thick and fluffy. If desired, fold in vanilla, liqueur, or orange or lemon zest. Serve either hot or cold in glasses.

Ada Boni, Italian Regional Cooking

*Opposite: Banchetto, Marcello Fogolino (1470–c. 1550).
Castello, Malpaga (detail)*

NAture c̄ ī q̊ . ſ. īƺ. Melius exeis modice acui
tatis. Iuuamentum toſieis. Nocumentum ex
pulſiue & cerebro. Remotio nocumenti cum aceto
ſis & oleo.

March

26
27
28
29
1
2
3

What do you think?
Young women of rank
actually eat — you will never
guess what — garlick!

Percy Bysshe Shelley (1792-1822)

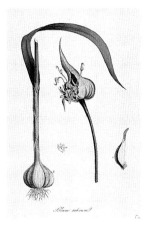

Pesto, the traditional sauce of Genoa, is a compound of garlic, basil, olive oil, ewe's milk cheese, and pine nuts or walnuts.

Piedmont is the home of bagna cauda, a hot garlic and anchovy dip for vegetables.

BRUSCHETTA
Toast sliced Italian bread until crisp, brush with olive oil, rub with crushed garlic, sprinkle with salt and freshly ground pepper, and serve immediately.

Ada Boni, Italian Regional Cooking

Opposite: illumination from Tacuinum Sanitatis de Sex Rebus, Ibn Botlan. Bibliotheque Municipale, Rouen, France

I frutti proibiti sono i più dolci.

Stolen fruit is the sweetest.

4	
5	
6	1475 b. Caprese—Michelangelo Buonarotti, sculptor, painter, architect, and poet
7	
8	
9	
10	

FAIRER THAN TURNIP

Oh, your face is much sweeter than mustard,
Fairer than turnip. A snail has pushed its vehicle
On it, and made it as it is—so lustered.
Your teeth are parsnip-white, and your sweet giggle
Would doubtless turn the Pope's heart into custard.
Your eyes are just as colorful as treacle,
Your hair is blond and white like bulbs of leeks:
Oh make me alive! That's all my spirit seeks.

> Michelangelo, The Complete Poems of Michelangelo
> Translated by Joseph Tusiani

CASTANI DI LUCIFERO

LUCIFER'S CHESTNUTS

❧ Take forty good chestnuts and roast them over a
slow fire. Do not allow them to become dried up or
colored. Remove the shells carefully, put them in a
bowl, and pour over them one-half a glass of rum and
two or three tablespoons of powdered sugar. Set fire
to the rum and baste the chestnuts constantly as long
as the rum will burn, turning the chestnuts about so
they will absorb the rum and become colored.

> Antonia Isola, Simple Italian Cookery

Above: Canestro di frutta, Caravaggio (1573–1610), *Pinacoteca Ambrosiana, Milano*

Opposite: Vertumnus (Emperor Rudolph II), *Giuseppe Archimboldo (1527–1593). Skoklosters Slott, Sweden*

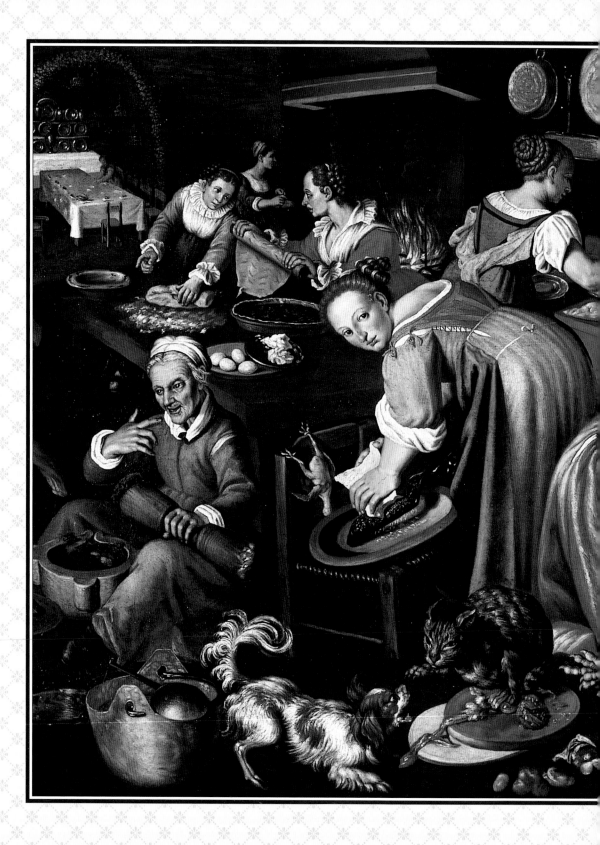

A Feast Prepared for Pope Pius V by Bartolomeo Scappi—1570

FIRST COURSE—Cold Delicacies from the Sideboard

Pieces of marzipan and marzipan balls * Neapolitan spice cakes * Malaga wine and Pisan biscuits * Plain pastries made with milk and eggs * Fresh grapes * Spanish olives * Prosciutto cooked in wine, sliced, and served with capers, grape pulp, and sugar * Salted pork tongues cooked in wine, sliced * Spit-roasted songbirds, cold, with their tongues sliced over them * Sweet mustard

SECOND COURSE—Roasts

Fried veal sweetbreads and liver, with a sauce of eggplant, salt, sugar, and pepper * Spit-roasted skylarks with lemon sauce * Spit-roasted quails with sliced aubergines * Stuffed spit-roasted pigeons with sugar and capers sprinkled over them * Spit-roasted rabbits, with sauce and crushed pine nuts * Partridges, larded and spit-roasted, served with lemon slices * Pastries filled with minced veal sweetbreads and served with plices of prosciutto * Strongly seasoned poultry with lemon slices and sugar * Slices of veal, spit-roasted, with a sauce made from the juices * Leg of goat, spit-roasted, with a sauce made from the juices * Soup of almond cream, with the flesh of three pigeons for every two guests * Squares of meat aspic

THIRD COURSE—Boiled Meats and Stews

Stuffed fat geese, boiled Lombard style and covered with sliced almonds, served with cheese, sugar, and cinnamon * Stuffed breast of veal, boiled, garnished with flowers * Milk calf, boiled, garnished with parsley * Almonds in garlic sauce * Turkish-style rice with milk, sprinkled with sugar and cinnamon * Stewed pigeons with mortadella sausage and whole onions * Cabbage soup with sausages * Poultry pie, two chickens to each pie * Fricasseed breast of goat dressed with fried onions * Pied filled with custard cream * Boiled calves' feet with cheese and egg

FOURTH COURSE—Delicacies from the Sideboard

Bean tarts * Quince pastries, one quince per pastry * Pear tarts, the pears wrapped in marzipan * Parmesan cheese and Riviera cheese * Fresh almonds on vine leaves * Chestnuts roasted over the coals and served with salt, sugar, and pepper * Milk curds with sugar sprinkled over * Ring-shaped cakes * Wafers

La Cucina, Vincenzo Campi (1536-1591). Pinacoteca di Brera, Milano

11	
12	
13	
14	～ Olives produced in different regions show a wide variety of color, size, and flavor. When bought, store them in a glass jar, covered with olive oil, in a dark place. ～ Elizabeth David, Italian Food OLIVE OIL ～ Olive oil, the crucial ingredient of Italian cooking, has been prized in Italy since the days of the Romans—Virgil and Ovid wrote in praise of the olive tree, its fruit and oil. Olive trees grow principally along the coast, from the south to Liguria, and are harvested in the fall. ～ Vogue Entertaining
15	
Ides of March	
16	
17	
ancient Roman festival honoring all the gods	Opposite: Copyright Museo Nazionale delle Paste Alimentari

Winter's grip has relaxed, and spring's quickening winds are welcome back.

Horace, Odes

18

19

ancient Roman festival—rededication of Minerva's temple
St. Joseph's Day (Italy)

20

43 B.C. b. Ovid, Roman poet

21

equinox

22

23

24

ancient Roman day of mourning and abstinence

It is quite clear that the body must be recognised and the soul kept in its place, since a little refreshing food and drink can do so much to make a man.

Hilaire Belloc, The Path to Rome, 1902

LE DOLCEZZE (THE SWEETNESSES)
The sky-blue Sundays of spring.
The snow on top of the houses like a white wig.
The lovers' walks along the canal.
Making bread on Sunday mornings.
The rain in March that beats on the gray rooftops.
  Corrado Govoni

Gaé. Mitelli Inu. H Curti fe.

Vieni: di questo cascio haurai buon saggio,
Se uorrai saporir dolci beuande
Se uorrai regallar, condir uiuande,
Non ti dispiaccia il piacentin formaggio.

25

26

27

28

29

30

31

〜 Mozzarella is traditionally made from the milk of the domesticated Asian water buffalo and worked by hand. Nowadays, powdered milk or cow's milk is often used. 〜

Paul Hoffman, That Fine Italian Hand

〜 *Most Italians believe cheeses should be eaten in the area from which they come: ricotta in Rome, Fontina in Piedmont, mozzarella in Naples, Parmesan in Parma and Reggio.* 〜

World Atlas of Food

Opposite: Venditore di formaggio, *Giuseppe Maria Mitelli (1634–1718). Biblioteca Nazionale, Firenze*

April

1	
2	
3	
4	
5	
6	
1483 b. Raphael, painter	
1520 d. Raphael, painter	
1748 ruins of Pompeii discovered	
7	

PRAISE TO MACARONI

Beautiful and white
As you emerge in groups
Out of the machine
If on a cloth
You are made to lie
You look to me like the milky way.

Zounds!
Great Desire,
Master of this earthly life,
I waste away,
I faint from the wish
To taste you
O maccheroni!

Filippo Sagruttendio, from Le Laude de Li
Maccarune (Praise to Macaroni), *Naples 1646*

Spaghetti a "Cacio e pepe"

Spaghetti with cheese and pepper

❧ Bring a large pan of salted water to a fast boil.
Slowly add the spaghetti (1½ pounds) and cook until
just tender. Drain in a colander, but not too thoroughly. Serve immediately with freshly ground black
pepper and ¾ cup Pecorino cheese. As the spaghetti
would be far too dry with simply the pepper and
cheese dressing, the cooking water which adheres to
it is allowed to remain to keep it moist. Sometimes a
little oil, or lightly fried pork fat or bacon is added
but this is not traditional. Serves 6

Ada Boni, Italian Regional Cooking

How fair is youth, and how fast it flies away.
Let him who will be merry, of tomorrow nothing is certain.

Lorenzo de Medici, fifteenth century

8

1492 d. Lorenzo de Medici, Florentine ruler and arts patron

9

10

11

12

13

14

PASTIERA

NEAPOLITAN EASTER PIE

For the pastry:
2¼ cups flour * 1 cup sugar
¾ cup butter * 3 egg yolks
confectioners' sugar

For the filling:
10 oz ricotta * 1⅓ cup sugar
4 egg yolks * 4 oz candied citron and orange
3 tbsp orange water * 4 egg whites, beaten
8 oz (after soaking), dried corn soaked in cold water
for 2 or 3 days * ½ qt milk
rind of ½ lemon, whole * ½ tsp vanilla
½ tsp cinnamon * salt

✄ To make the pastry, blend the flour and butter and add the egg yolks. Blend well and add a little tepid water if necessary. Cover and chill the dough in the refrigerator for an hour. To prepare the filling, drain the soaked corn and cook it in a covered pan with the milk, lemon rind, and a pinch of salt. Cook over low heat until it is thick and creamy, then add the vanilla and cinnamon to the mixture. Pour it into a bowl and remove the lemon rind. In another bowl mix the ricotta with the sugar, the candied citron and orange rind, the egg yolks, orange water and the corn. Then add the beaten egg whites. Roll the pastry out into two rounds, one slightly larger than the other. Line a baking pan with the pastry and pour the filling into the pastry shell. Cut the remaining pastry into strips and arrange them on the pastiera in a lattice pattern. Cook in a hot oven at about 180°C/350°F until the filling looks dry and the pastry is browned. Let it cool in the pan, sprinkling with confectioners' sugar.

Giusy Gallo, Italy, Italy

Opposite: The Marriage at Cana, Paolo Veronese (1528–1588). Musée du Louvre, Paris (detail)

All roads lead to Rome.

Jean de la Fontaine

15

1452 b. Vinci—Leonardo da Vinci, artist and inventor

16

17

18

19

20

21

traditionally, last year's wine first tested in ancient Rome

753 B.C. Legend says that today Romulus founded the City of Rome on seven hills overlooking the Tiber River.

Oh Rome! my country! city of the soul!

Byron

Cappelletti alla Romagna

1 cup ricotta ∗ ½ half breast capon, sautéed in butter, seasoned with salt and pepper, and finely chopped ∗ 2 or 3 tablespoons grated Parmesan cheese ∗ 1 egg and 1 yolk ∗ a little nutmeg, grated lemon rind, and any other spices you may desire ∗ salt to taste ∗ (Lean pork loin or breast of chicken may be substituted for capon.)
✣ Mix the above ingredients and taste, adding more seasoning, if necessary. If the ricotta is very soft the egg white may be omitted, and if it is very dry 2 whole eggs may be used. Beat 2 [more] eggs well. Add enough flour to make rather a stiff dough. Knead well and roll thin. With a cookie cutter about 2 inches diameter cut into discs. Put a little of the above mixture into each and fold over in half, pressing the edges together. If you have difficulty making the edges stick together dip the finger-tips into cold water, rub along the inside edge and press together. Boil the cappelletti in chicken broth and serve hot. Parmesan cheese may be added, if desired. Serve 10 to 15 cappelletti to each portion. Cappelletti may also be taken out of the broth, seasoned with butter and Parmesan and served as a separate dish.
Alberto Alfani, One Hundred Genuine Italian Recipes

Opposite: Carta del Mediterraneo, 14th century. Private collection, Padova

22	
23	
24	
25 Feast of St. Mark, Venice Liberation Day (Italy) Anzac Day (Australia and New Zealand)	
26	
27	
28	

UP AT A VILLA—DOWN IN THE CITY

The house for me, no doubt, were a house
    in the city-square;
Ah, such a life, such a life, as one leans at
    the window there!
Something to see, by Bacchus, something
    to hear, at least!
There, the whole day long, one's life is a
    perfect feast...
    Robert Browning

There are several indigenous Abruzzi liqueurs, one of which has to be drunk in order not to believe it. Could anything be quite so strong?
    Edward Harvane, East of Rome: A Journey
    into the Abruzzi

May

29	
30	
1 Labor Day (Italy)	
2	
3	
4	
5	

In the nineteenth century, street vendors sold spaghetti from wooden vats over charcoal fires—patrons ate it with their hands.

Lorenza de Medici, Heritage of Italian Cooking

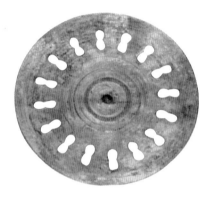

THE ORIGINS OF PASTA

From as early as the eleventh century, Italian pasta (originally known generically as "macaroni") spread through the country from the great port cities—noodles had already reached India and the Arab lands before Marco Polo was even born. In India and the Middle East, noodles were called, respectively, sevika and rishta, meaning "thread;" the Italian word spaghetti derives from spago, or "string." Naples is now the center of pasta making.

Reay Tannahill, Food in History

The Apulians are the greatest pasta eaters in Italy. The quintessential Apulian pasta is orecchiette—little shells.

Ada Boni, Italian Regional Cooking

TRATTORIA.

*Old Capulet: Look to the bak'd meats, good Angelica.
Spare not for the cost.*

William Shakespeare, Romeo and Juliet

6	
7	
8	
9	
10	
11	
12	

WILD BOAR

Here, then, we ate wild boar, shot in the precincts of the mine that very morning, and baked in a ground oven by a Sarde cook. With lettuces, bread, cheese, olives, oranges, wine of Tortoli, and the mountain air, it was a feast for an alderman.

Charles Edwards, Sardinia and the Sardes, 1889

A specialty of Umbria is porchetta—pork belly stuffed with herbs and fennel; from Modena comes zamponi—pigs' feet stuffed with pork. Such rich meat dished belie the idea that Italian cooking is little but pasta-and-sauces.

H.V. Morton, A Traveller in Italy

OSSO BUCO

Select four pieces of veal shank cut in size for individual serving. In a deep kettle melt about 2 tablespoons or more of butter. To this add a small onion, 1 carrot and 1 or 2 stalks celery, all minced very fine. Put the veal shanks in this and let them brown well on all sides. When brown add more butter—about the same quantity as before—and a rounded tablespoonful of flour. Blend well, season with salt and pepper and a bayleaf, and add 4 ounces of dry white wine. Add enough hot water to cover the meat and simmer slowly for three or four hours. As the gravy simmers away turn the pieces of meat gently so as to cook evenly on all sides, but try not to break it away from the bones. A few minutes before serving place the meat in a casserole, strain the sauce over it, sprinkle with finely chopped parsley, grated lemon rind and a clove of garlic minced. Let stand covered a few minutes and serve.

Alberto Alfani, One Hundred Genuine Italian Recipes

Opposite: Still Life II, Jacopo da Empoli. Uffizi, Firenze (detail)

Venice is like eating an entire box of chocolate liqueurs in one go.

Truman Capote

13

1931 Harry's Bar, Venice, opened

14

15

ancient Roman festival honoring Mercury

16

17

18

19

---

*Venice! he who never saw
you cannot prize you;
he who has seen too much
of you must despise you!*

Italian proverb

Napoleon said the Piazza San Marco was the best drawing room in Europe; I would nominate Harry's as one of the two or three best saloons.
Jan Morris, The Harry's Bar Cookbook

*A Venezia chi vi nasce,
mal vi si pasce.*

He who is born at Venice is badly fed there.
Venetian proverb

A cask of wine works more miracles than a church full of saints.

Italian proverb

20

feast of St. Bernardine of Siena

Victoria Day (Canada)

21

ancient Roman festival honoring all the gods

22

23

24

25

26

In a Field of Siena

Young girl that in the field hast work begun,
And with thy great straw hat dost seem the sun,
Fair thief-of-hearts they call thee, every one.

Tuscan folk rhyme

CHIANTI

The classic Italian wine Chianti is produced in Tuscany: only the wines that come from Arezzo, Pisa, Pistoia, and Siena can be sold as chianti classico. The wine is usually sold as soon as it is ready, at the age of six months or so, though it is at its best after five to eight years of aging. It is made from a blend of grapes, but Sangiovese grapes usually comprise about 70–90 percent.

Lidia Bastianich and Jay Jacobs, La Cucina di Lidia

June

27	
28	
29	
30	
31	
1	
2	

Republic Day (Italy)

**SE DONO. VITA, TU SEI
(LIFE, IF YOU ARE A GIFT)**
Life, if you are
the gift of remote Gods,
why do we consume you thus,
oh not like sweet fruit
that is the fragrance of springs
and restores us after dark winters.
Sibilla Aleramo

MINESTRA CELESTIALE

HEAVENLY SOUP

❧ Beat the yolks of 3 eggs until lemon colored and
fold in the stiffly beaten whites of three eggs. Pour
this over a mixture of very fine, dried bread crumbs.
Add about three tablespoons of grated Parmesan
cheese and a dash of ground nutmeg. Mix gently so
that the batter will remain soft. Drop by teaspoonfuls
into boiling broth and let boil 7 or 8 minutes. Serve
piping hot, with a few of these "dumplings" to each
serving. More Parmesan cheese may be added to the
soup, if desired.

Alberto Alfani, One Hundred Genuine Italian Recipes

Opposite: illumination from Codice Officium Beatae Virginis,
giugno, la miet itura. Biblioteca Civica, Forli'

d	xi	kl'	
c	x	kl'	sci paulun epi 7 9f.
f	viiii	kl'	
g	viii	kl'	nat sci johis baptiste.
a	vii	kl'	
b	vi	kl'	scoz. m. johis et pauli.
c	v	kl'	
d	iiii	kl'	sci leonis. p̄p̄. 7 9f.
e	iii	kl'	scoz aplox petri et pauli.
f	ii	kl'	comemoratio sci pauli.

E porci morti e fenissimi cochi, / Ghiotti morselli, ciascun bea e mandochi...

And whole dead pigs, and cunning cooks to ply / Each throat with tit-bits that shall satisfy...
Folgore da San Gemignano (c. A.D. 13–14) Translated by Dante Gabriel Rossetti

3

4

5

6

7

8

9

UOVE SODE GROSSE

LARGE HARDBOILED EGGS

An egg as big as the head of a man may be made in this manner. Separate the yolks from the whites of twenty-five eggs, and beat the yolks well with a whisk, one at a time. The well-beaten yolks are put into pig's bladder; the bladder is sealed and immersed in a boiler full of boiling water until the yolks are quite firm. This great hardboiled yolk is then removed from the bladder and placed in another much larger one, which already contains the stiffly beaten whites of the eggs, and this is then sealed, taking care that the yolk is well covered by the whites. The bladder is tied up with string and dangled in the boiling water until the eggwhite hardens; then this last bladder is also removed, leaving a huge hardboiled egg.

Vincenzo Tanara, L'Economia del Cittadino in Villa (Economy in the City Home), 1687

PASTICCIO DI UCCELLI VIVI

PIE WITH LIVE BIRDS

You can make a pie with live birds in the following manner. First, make a pastry casing and fill it with bran, and after you have covered it put it on to cook. When it has cooked and thoroughly cooled, make a small hole in the bottom to take out the bran, and put in a few live small birds and plenty of leaves from a tree. Then put the piece of pastry you took out to make the hole back in exactly the same position. And be sure to make several tiny holes on top so that the little birds will not suffocate for want of air. The you set the abovementioned pie before some gentlemen and ladies, if you wish to have a little fun, and when they open the pie the above-mentioned birds will fly away.

Anonymous, Liber de Coquina (Book of Cooking), fifteenth century

Opposite: Market scene, fresco (late 15th century). Castello di Issogne, Val d'Aosta (detail)

10	
11	
12	
13	
feast of St. Anthony of Padua	
14	
15	
16	

STRACCIATELLA

EGG AND CHEESE SOUP—a specialty of the Rome-Lazio region

3 eggs
salt
4 tablespoons semolina
4 tablespoons grated Parmesan cheese
freshly grated nutmeg (optional)
7½ cups meat stock

❧ Beat the eggs in a bowl with a good pinch of salt, the semolina, Parmesan cheese, and grated nutmeg to taste. Dilute the mixture with a ladleful of cold stock. Bring the remaining stock to the boil, pour in the egg mixture and stir thoroughly, using a wire whisk. Lower the heat and simmer for 2 minutes, beating constantly. Serve boiling hot, with the beaten egg just breaking up into strands.

Lidia Bastianich and Jay Jacobs, La Cucina di Lidia

SCAROLA AFFOGATA

SMOTHERED ESCAROLE—popular throughout Italy: spinach or other leafy greens can be prepared the same way

1 pound (2 medium heads) escarole
6 cloves garlic, crushed
3 tablespoons olive oil
½ teaspoon salt
¼ teaspoon hot red pepper flakes
fresh black pepper, 4 twists of the mill

❧ Remove the outer leaves of the escarole if they are damaged or discolored. Cut off the bases, wash the leaves twice in abundant cold water, and drain. In a large pot, sauté the garlic in the oil until it is golden but not brown. Add the remaining ingredients, cover, and cook over moderate heat 3–4 minutes, stirring occasionally. Remove and discard the garlic, serve immediately.

Lidia Bastianich and Jay Jacobs, La Cucina di Lidia

Opposite: The Summer, *Giuseppe Archimboldo (1527-1593)*

Now the forest is clothed with verdure,
Now the year is at its most beautiful.

Virgil, Eclogues

17

18

19

20

21

22

solstice

23

PROCIUTTO DI PARMA

Prosciutto di Parma (Parma ham) should be pale red in color, mild, tender, and sweet. It should be served cut into very thin slices, with chunks of melon or fresh figs.

Elizabeth David, Italian Food

THE VERY FIRST COOKBOOK

The very first cookbook was written by a Roman named Celius Apicius, probably in A.D. 230. Apicius gathered contemporary recipes (including one for prosciutto cooked in honey with dried figs and bay leaves) and wrote some of his own.

Lorenza de Medici,
The Heritage of Italian Cooking

All' amico curagli il fico,
all' inimico il persico.

Pull a fig for your friend,
and a peach for your enemy.

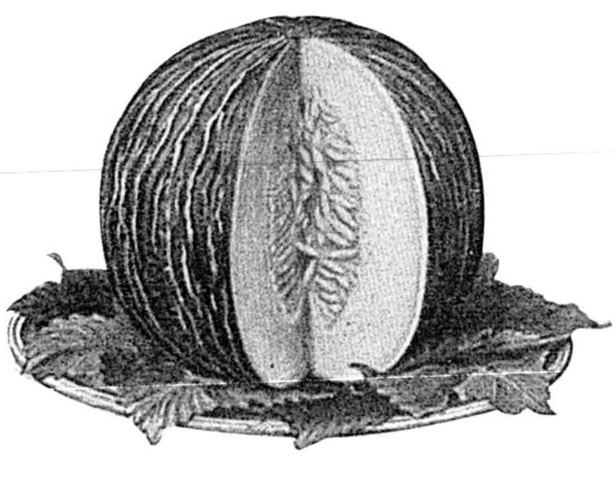

Opposite: Figs, Bartolomeo Bimbi. Galleria Palatina, Palazzo Pitti, Firenze

Fichi Settentrini
1. Albi.
2. Rossettini dell'Vnigiana
3. Verdini Bianchi
4. Dotrati saluatici d'Aug.
5. Pisanello
6. Brogiotto Bianco
7. Lardello
8. Garaocuio
9. S. Maria
10. Brogiotto Romano
11. Sampiero
12. Castagniolo
13. Verdino
14. Cutrolo
15. Cetri
16. Garbuio
17. Piroli
18. Pessciuni
19. Ottieri
20. Dottati
21. Brogiotti
22. Verdoni
23. Lardaioli
24. Rondone Pisto
Corbolini
Pedron Rossi

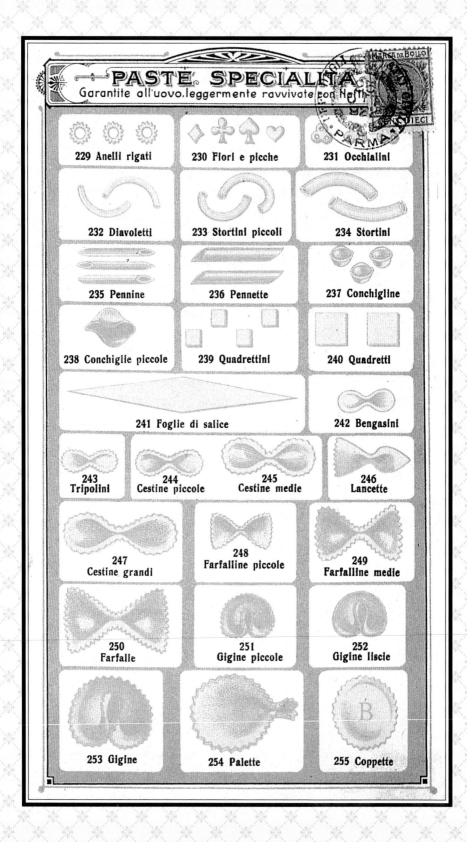

PASTE SPECIALITÀ
Garantite all'uovo, leggermente ravvivate con Naftha

229 Anelli rigati

230 Fiori e picche

231 Occhialini

232 Diavoletti

233 Stortini piccoli

234 Stortini

235 Pennine

236 Pennette

237 Conchigline

238 Conchiglie piccole

239 Quadrettini

240 Quadretti

241 Foglie di salice

242 Bengasini

243 Tripolini

244 Cestine piccole

245 Cestine medie

246 Lancette

247 Cestine grandi

248 Farfalline piccole

249 Farfalline medie

250 Farfalle

251 Gigine piccole

252 Gigine lische

253 Gigine

254 Palette

255 Coppette

24	**AN ODE TO MACARONI**

As I entered the door, I smelled
the aroma of ragù.
So…Take care…Goodbye…
I am leaving…If I sit
I might not go… |
| 25 | I am sure it is macaroni
I heard cracking
As I entered the door.
Could it be? |
| 26 | A tomato skin is resting on your arm
like a blood stain…Permit me?
I will remove it!
How fine your skin feels…
like silk, slipping under my fingers… |
| 27 | You look especially beautiful this morning.
Your face reflects fire…
I am sure it's the macaroni… |
| 28 | I am going…Goodbye!
If I sit, I might not leave…
I might wait
'til you sit at the table,
to receive a ragù-flavored kiss!
Rocco Galdieri, from "Sunday," Naples, 1932 |

MACARONI ALLA QUARESIMA

❧ Parboil twelve ounces of macaroni and drain it well. Put one onion, a little parsley, and six anchovies all finely chopped up, into a frying pan with butter, and fry for six or eight minutes; add this to the macaroni with half a tumbler of white wine, one of fish stock (or water), and a pinch of white pepper, boil over a slow fire for twenty minutes, and serve at once sprinkled with grated Parmesan cheese.

Janet Ross, Leaves from Our Tuscan Kitchen

29

Saints Peter and Paul Day | |
| 30 | |

July

1	
2	
3	
4 Independence Day (USA)	
5	
6	
7	

La prima oliva e oro,
la seconda argento,
la terza non
val niente.

The best olive is gold, the second silver,
the third is worth nothing.
Tuscan saying

JULY

For July, in Siena, by the willow tree,
    I give you barrels of white Tuscan wine
    In ice far down your cellars stored supine;
And morn and eve to eat in company
Of those vast jellies dear to you and me;
    Of partridges and youngling pheasants sweet,
    Boiled capons, sovereign kids: and let their treat
Be veal and garlic, with whom these agree.
Let time slip by, till by-and-by, all day;
    And never swelter through the heat at all,
But move at ease at home, sound, cool, and gay;
    And wear sweet-colored robes that lightly fall;
And keep your tables set in fresh array,
Not coaxing spleen to be your seneschal.
    Folgore a San Gemignana (c. A.D. 13–14)
    Translated by Dante Gabriel Rossetti

Opposite: Natura morta con frutta, Vincenzo Campi
(1536–1591). Pinacoteca di Brera, Milano (detail)

8	
9	
10	
11	
12	
13	
14	

RISOTTO

∽ Rice and polenta are staples in northern Italy. Risottos are made with short-grain Arborio rice, which is sautéed in butter, then simmered in stock or water—often with some white wine—for 15 to 20 minutes or until the rice is al dente. ∽

World Atlas of Food

MINESTRA DI BOMBOLINE DI RISO

SOUP WITH RICE DUMPLINGS

½ cup rice
1½ cupfuls milk
1 tablespoon butter
2 tablespoons grated Parmesan cheese
1 egg yolk
dash nutmeg
salt to taste

❀ Boil or steam the potatoes with skins on. Peel, mash and add salt. Mix with all the other above ingredients. Sprinkle a little flour on a baking board and place the above mixture on this in long strips so that they may be rolled in the flour without any of the flour getting on the inside. The rolls should be about ½ inch in diameter. Cut these strips into ½ inch pieces and make balls. Fry these in deep hot olive oil, drain well. Serve with additional Parmesan cheese, if desired.

Alberto Alfani, One Hundred Genuine Italian Recipes

Opposite: illumination from Codice Officium Beatae Virginis, iuglio, la batt itura. Biblioteca Civica, Forli'

f xij kl' scē praxedis urrg.
g xj kl' scē magdalene.
A x kl' sci apolonaris epi q̄m.
b viij kl' scē cristine urrg q̄m.
c viij kl' sci jacobi apli scī xp̄o fori m̄
d vij kl' sci pastoris q̄f' q̄ scē anne.
e vj kl' scōr. m̄. pateleonis
f v kl' scōr. m̄. nazary q̄ inocetī.
g iiij kl' scōr. m̄. felicis et beatricis.
A iij kl' scōr. m̄. abdon et senen.
b ij kl'.

O Francia o Spagna, purché si magna.

It matters not who rules us, so long as we eat.
Neapolitan saying

15	
16	
17	
18	
19	
20	
21	

The word "pizza" derives from the Latin picea, "of pitch," which probably refers to the texture or color of the baked pie. Pizza probably appeared in Naples around 500 B.C.

Paul Hoffman, That Fine Italian Hand

FRITTO DI MOZZARELLA

FRIED MOZZARELLA CHEESE
olive oil for deep frying
3 eggs
salt
12 slices mozzarella or Scamorza cheese, ½ inch thick (about 1½ pounds)
flour
fine breadcrumbs

❧ Heat plenty of olive oil in a deep pan. Beat the eggs with a pinch of salt. Coat the cheese slices with flour, dip them in the beaten eggs, roll in breadcrumbs and then dip once again in beaten eggs. Drop a few at a time into the hot oil. As soon as the cheese is golden brown, take it from the pan with a perforated spoon and drain on paper towels. Serve immediately.

Ada Boni, Italian Regional Cooking

Rissole alla Napoletana

Neapolitan fritters

❈ Chop two fresh buffalo cheeses, add a little Parmesan, some *marzolino* and some grated *caciocavallo* [a cheese originally made from sheep's milk], and a slice of prosciutto which you have chopped and sweated a little in a saucepan over the fire, some chopped parsley, some crushed pepper, nutmeg, two uncooked eggs, and mix all these well together. Roll out a sheet of short pastry made with butter or lard (it matters little which) to a thickness of one *paolo* [an old coin], make little mounds of the above mixture on it and brush some beaten egg all around each one, then fold the dough back over the top, seal it well and cut it with a fluted pastry cutter into small half-moon-shaped *ravioli*. At serving time, fry them in very hot pork fat and serve them as soon as they are nice and golden. In Naples these fritters, which we call *rissole*, are known as *panzarotti*.

Francesco Leonardi, L'Apicio Moderno
(The Modern Apicius), 1790

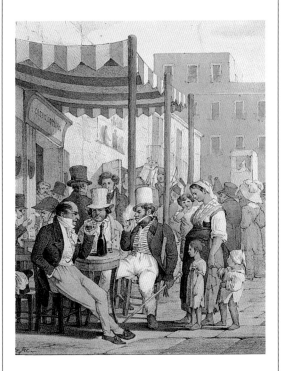

Zuppa di erbe alla Napoletana

Neapolitan herb soup

❈ The area around Naples is so beautiful and well cultivated that it gives more than a little pleasure to anyone to gaze upon it, and all the herbs that are produced there have the sweetest taste, so that the Neapolitans never boil them to make soups, except for chicory, cardoons and a few other species. Moreover, it is true that in the kitchens of the great are served soups of herbs boiled and arranged in bunches or otherwise, and the most flavorsome way is to put them uncooked into the broth, either alone or several kinds mixed together. Certainly the soup will not have the symmetry one would wish in the tureen, but that will be compensated for by the excellent flavor and taste of the herbs that are cooked in the broth. Furthermore, everyone can prepare the herbs to his own taste.

Francesco Leonardi, L'Apicio Moderno
(The Modern Apicius), 1790

Whose bread and cheese I eat, to his tune I dance.

Florentine saying

22	
23	
24	
25	
26	
27	
28	

THE MOST DELICATE FOOD

⁓ Butter is held as the most delicate food among barbarous nations, and one which distinguishes the wealthy from the multitude at large. ⁓

Pliny the elder

⁓ In Calabria, they make a sort of bread called pitte, which are "painted" with a variety of ingredients from tomatoes and peppers to sardines to herbs. Pitte were once the ritual food of one of the many civilizations that invaded the shores of Calabria in ancient times. ⁓

Ada Boni, Italian Regional Cooking

Opposite: The Summer, Giuseppe Archimboldo (1527–1593).

August

29	
30	
31	
1	
2	
3	
4	

A famous dish of Messina is pescespada a ghiotta: swordfish baked in pastry with onion, tomato, capers, celery, olives, and potatoes.

World Atlas of Food

Above: Cooking. Detail of lunette, Federigo Zuccaro. Palazzetto di Federico Zuccari, Firenze

La Tinca

TENCH

❧ I believe the fish that today is known as tench was at one time called *mena*. If it is large and you wish to cook it by boiling, eat it dressed with verjuice, spices, and very finely chopped parsley, or, again if it is large, after you have removed the scales cut it along the backbone, turn it inside out so that its innards are on the outside, remove the entrails and bones and put in a mixture made from its eggs, chopped parsley, crushed pepper and garlic and a little saffron. There are some who make this mixture with black or red cherries or with sultanas, shelled pine nuts and a beaten egg. Finally, cook it over the coals on low heat, and as soon as it is cooked dress it with some vinegar pickle and oil, and moisten with verjuice or orange juice. Whatever way you cook it, there is nothing worse than tench.

Bartolomeo Platina, De Honesta Voluptate
ac Valetudine (Concerning Honest Pleasure
and Well-being), 1474

PESCE A CAPPUCCIOLO

FISH IN A CLOAK

❧ Of all the varieties of fish, I find *meggia* [dialect name for grey mullet], gild-head sea bream, medium dentex, river perch and grayling are good cooked by this method which is called *cappucciolo*. You shall take one of the aforementioned fish and split it down the back and take out the innards, then you put it to soak in some vinegar and wine and salt and powdered coriander or crushed fennel seeds. Let it remain in the vinegar and wine bath just described for three or four hours, but no more than this. Then give it a good wash and dredge it lightly in flour and thread it onto a spit, and put it on to cook, turning the spit a little bit one way and a little bit the other way, that is to say a little turn of the point of the skewer and a little turn of the handle. When it is cooked you shall take some shelled walnuts, hardboiled egg yolks, raisins, and a little honey or sugar and some parsley and mint, and pound all this together, moistening every ingredient with verjuice. This you shall pass through a sieve, and then set it to boil in a saucepan so that it thickens a little. Then when you have opened up the fish, put this sauce on top of it. When you do not wish to go to the expense of this sauce, you shall use instead vinegar and parsley.

Cristoforo di Messisbugo, Banchetti Composizioni di
Vivande e Apparecchio Generale (Banquets,
Composition of Meals and General Equipment),
sixteenth century

Fig. 699. Jégle, luciae, sardae.

Fig. 68. Carps, anguilly, brochet.

5

6

7

8

9

10

11

PESCE CON VINO

PEACHES WITH WINE

⌘ Take four very ripe peaches, cut them in two, take out the stones, peel them, and cut them in thin slices. Put them in a bowl and cover them up until wanted. Put in a saucepan one glass of red wine, two table-spoons of powdered sugar, a piece of cinnamon, and a piece of a rind of a lemon. Boil these together, and then pour the liquid over the peaches in the bowl while still boiling. Cover the bowl, and allow it to stand for at least two hours. Then turn into the dish in which you will serve the peaches and the wine.

Antonia Isola, Simple Italian Cookery

BEANS COOKED IN A WINE FLASK

〜 An ancient, traditional Tuscan dish is fagioli nel fiasco, beans cooked in a flask. In a chianti bottle, white beans are cooked with olive oil, sage, garlic, and water on special braziers over charcoal fires for several hours. 〜

Ada Boni, Italian Regional Cooking

Homecomings

Hands clasped under my head/I recalled the times I returned, the smell of fruit drying on hurdles,/of wallflowers, lavender, ginger
Salvatore Quasimodo

12	**CORSICAN SCENES** The market stalls were all up, the booths filled with melons, peaches, grapes, tomatoes, aubergines. The scents mingled and spread across the streets in heavy woven nets of perfume.
13	Up on the hillside, through a pergola of vine and figs, the small lights of the restaurant played out over flower beds and stone verandahs. On the tables were tomatoes, lobsters, whiting, great bowls of soup, cheese and wine.
14	Lower down the natural means of life are laid, wine in green glasses, grapes, and silver fishes; clay pipes like targets stick from olive vases, and corals glow with sunsets in pale dishes.
15 *Assumption*	*Quotes from Alan Ross,* Time was Away: A Journey through Corsica
16	
17	
18	*Opposite: Still life with cherries, Bartolomeo Bimbi. Uffizi, Firenze*

Acqua e pane, vita da cane.

Bread and water are fit for a dog.

Italian proverb

19

20

21

22

23

ancient Roman festival honoring Vulcan, god of fire

A.D. 79 Mount Vesuvius erupts, destroying Pompeii and Herculaneum in two days

24

25

In Sardinia, bread is a symbol of family unity.
World Atlas of Food

PANE SPEZIALE ALLA BRESCIANA

BRESCIA SPICED BREAD

❉ Take one pound of pure wheaten flour, one pound of sugar, half a pound of butter, a little warm water, and form these into a dough that is just a little softer than short pastry; shape it into a cake, then fill it with the following stuffing. Take one pound of blanched almonds and pound them in a mortar with the white of an egg, then put them into a dish and add one pound of whole pine nuts, mixing in also one pound of powdered sugar, two ounces of sweet spices, nine ounces of raisins, some chopped citron peel. Knead all this with a little must from the bottom of the wine cask and fill the cake with a little of this, then cover it with the dough, making some ornamentation or amusing decorations with the tip of a knife. Put it into the oven, and when it is baked place it on a serviette, dust the surface with sugar and serve.

Giovan Felice Luraschi, Milan,
nineteenth century

Above: Villa of Stabia, harbor of Pompeii, *fresco from a Stabian house (detail)*

Opposite: A baker shop, *fresco from Pompeii (detail)*

26	
27	
28	
29	
30	
31	
1	

GEORGIC

The time for setting vines is the first flush of spring
When that white bird arrives, the stork,
    the bane of serpents;
Or the first frosts of autumn,
    days when the hotfoot sun
Is not on winter's verge yet,
    but summer is now passing.
    Virgil
    Translated by C. Day Lewis

BALSAMIC VINEGAR

The best balsamic vinegar—so called because it is considered a balm—is made in Modena from the juice of the Trebbiano grape. The label "aceto balsamico tradizionale" means that the vinegar has aged five years in a wooden barrel.
    Lidia Bastianich and Jay Jacobs,
    La Cucina di Lidia

Opposite: illumination from Codice Officium Beatae Virginis, settembre, la vendemmia. Biblioteca Civica, Forli'

e	xi	kl'	sci marda apli en ig.
f	x	kl'	scox̃. m̃. maurici et focior̃ cuis.
g	viiij	kl'	sci linij. p̃. q̃iñ.
A	viij	kl'	scox̃. m̃. cypriam et ustine.
b	vij	kl'	scox̃. m̃. cofme et damiani.
c	vj	kl'	dedicatio sci michael' archangli.
d	v	kl'	sci ieronimi pbr̃.
e	iiij	kl'	
f	iij	kl'	
g	ij	kl'	

2	
3	
4	
5	
6	
7	
8	

SPEZIE (SPICES)

The great galleys of Venice and Florence
Be well laden with things of complacence;
All spicerye and of grocers ware
With sweet wines, all manner of fare…

> *Adam de Molyneux,*
> *Bishop of Chichester, fifteenth century*

OF SAFFRON

Saffron, 'tis said, brings comfort to mankind,
By giving rise to cheerfulness of mind.
Restores weak limbs, the liver also mends,
And normal vigor through its substance sends.

> *Regimen Sanitatis, 10th century*

Fiorentin mangia fagiuoli/ Lecca piatti e tovaglioli.

The Florentine who eats beans/ Licks the plates and tablecloths.
Florentine saying

9

10

11

12

13

14

15

FAGIOLI ALLA FIORENTINA

FLORENTINE BEANS

❧ Half-boil a quart of haricot beans in salted water, strain, and put them into a saucepan with some fried, browned butter in it. Mix, then drain off the butter, and add the following sauce: Melt four ounces of fresh butter, skim it carefully, add some flour and mix well, add some broth and stir until it is of the consistency of a sauce, and leave it to boil. Then pass the sauce through a sieve, put it back on the fire, and stir to prevent its sticking to the saucepan, add two yolks of eggs, the juice of half a lemon, and some finely chopped-up parsley. Pour the sauce over the beans before serving up hot.

Janet Ross, Leaves from Our Tuscan Kitchen

Above: Piatto di baccelli, *Giovanna Garzoni (1600–1670). Galleria Palatina, Firenze*

Opposite: Mangiatore di fagioli, *Annibale Carracci (1560–1609). Galleria Colonna, Roma*

Following pages: Storie di S. Barbara, *Lorenzo Lotto. Cappella Suardi, Trescore*

Everything you see, I owe to spaghetti.

Sophia Loren

16	
17	
18	
19	
20	
1934 b. Sophia Loren, actress	
21	
19 B.C. d. Virgil, poet	
22	

BEAUTIFUL MACARONI

Ceres, mother of Persephone
I have the urge
In my body,
Which torments me,
To sing
To praise
That which fills my stomach.

Bring me solace…
Help me, oh beautiful lady
Since I sing
The great glory
Of the beautiful macaroni…

> Filippo Sagruttendio, from Le Laude de Li
> Maccarune (Praise to Macaroni) Naples, 1646

Pappardelle con Lepre

❧ Make a paste with flour and three eggs, roll it about the thickness of a florin, and cut it into strips the width of a finger. Boil in salted water and put it aside to dry. Cut up the fillets, or the thighs of a hare (about eight ounces) into small pieces, mince one and a half ounces of bacon, half a small onion, half a carrot, and a quarter of a head of celery, and put them to cook with three-quarters of an ounce of butter, and season with salt and pepper. When browned, sprinkle the meat with one tablespoonful of flour, moisten it with one wine-glassful of gravy, and let it simmer for a time, adding one and a quarter ounces of butter and a little grated nutmeg. Place the pappardelle (the strips of paste) on a hot dish, grate a little Parmesan cheese over them, add the hare condiment, and serve hot.

> Janet Ross, Leaves from Our Tuscan Kitchen

Opposite: copyright Museo Nazionale delle Paste Alimentari

*Autumn, the bringer of fruit, has poured out her riches,
and soon sluggish winter returns.*

Horace, Odes

23 equinox	**CLASSIC GROUND** Wheresoe'er I turn my ravished eyes Gay gilded scenes and shining prospects rise. Poetic fields encompass me around And I still seem to travel on classic ground. 　　Joseph Addison (1701)

FRITTELLI DI CASTANO

CHESTNUT FRITTERS

❦ Take twenty good chestnuts and roast them on a slow fire so that they won't color. Remove the shells without breaking the nuts, and put them into a saucepan with one level tablespooon of powdered sugar and one-half glass of milk and a little vanilla. Cover the saucepan and let it cook slowly (simmer) for more than a half hour. Then drain the chestnuts and pass them through a sieve. Put them back in a bowl with one-half a tablespoon of butter, the yolks of three eggs, and mix well without cooking. Allow them to cool, and then take a small portion at a time, the size of a nut, roll them, dip them in egg, and in bread crumbs, and fry in butter, a few at a time. Serve hot with powdered sugar.

　Antonia Isola, Simple Italian Cookery

Separate calendar entries:

24

25

26

27

28

29

Opposite: Autumn, *Giuseppe Archimboldo (1527–1593).*
Musée du Louvre, Paris

October

30

1

2

3

4

5

6

Rape "armate"

"Reinforced" turnips

❧ Cook the turnips under the embers, or alternatively boil them whole when they are young and smooth and cut them into slices as thick as the blade of a knife; and you will have some good fat cheese cut into slices as large as the turnip slices, but thinner, and some sugar, some pepper and some sweet spices mixed together; put all this into a cake pan, set out in order on the bottom, first some slices of cheese to make the bottom crust, and on top of this you will put a layer of turnip, scattering over it the abovementioned spices, and plenty of good fresh butter; in this way you will gradually use up the turnips and the cheese until the pan is full; letting them cook for a quarter of an hour or more, like a cake. And this dish should be served after the others.

Maestro Martino da Como, Libro de Arte Coquinaria *(Book of Culinary Arts), fifteenth century*

Zucchi alla Fiorentina

Florentine-style Pumpkins

❧ Take twelve very young pumpkins (about one and a half inches long), cut them in half, and put them in cold water. Have a saucepan ready with four quarts of salted water. When boiling put in the pumpkins. When they are cooked put them again into cold water. Just before serving place them in a sauce-pan with four ounces of butter, heat for three minutes, then add two tablespoonfuls of veal broth, two of cream, and a squeeze of lemon. Heat again and serve.

Janet Ross, Leaves from Our Tuscan Kitchen

Opposite: illumination from Codice Officium Beatae Virginis, *ottobre, la raccolta delle rape. Biblioteca Civica, Forli'*

The First Italian Tomato Recipes

It was in 1781 that the first tomato recipe, Pomodori alla Certosina, was published—
by Vincenzo Corrado, a Celestine monk living in Naples.

7

8

9

10

1813 b. Giuseppe Verdi, composer

11

12
1492 Christopher Columbus (b. Genoa 1451) discovered the Americas and
so began the Columbian Exchange between the Old and the New Worlds—
only a few American plants spread to the New World but they included the
tomato, an indispensable item in many Italian dishes.

13

SALSA DI POMODORO

TOMATO SAUCE

❧ Finely chop ¼ onion, a clove of garlic, a piece of celery as long as a finger, some basil leaves, and as much parsley as you wish. Flavor with a bit of oil, salt, and pepper. Chop up seven or eight tomatoes and put everything in a pot. Cook, stirring from time to time, and when you see that the sauce has condensed into a thick cream, pass the purée through a sieve and serve. This sauce has many uses, as indicated in the various entries. It is good with boiled meats and excellent for flavoring pastas along with cheese and butter. And it is also good in preparing risotti.

Recipes from The Columbus Menu by Stefano Milioni

Pomodori alla Certosina

Tomatoes as prepared by the monks

❧ Fill the tomatoes with anchovy sauce, truffles, and the flesh of fish cooked in oil and pounded altogether and flavored with chopping greens. Fry the stuffed tomatoes in oil and serve them with puréed tomatoes.

〜 More than fifty years later, in 1839, Ippolito Cavalcanti, Duke of Buonvicino, wrote about Italy's most famous international dish, *spaghetti with tomato*, in *Cucina Casareccia in Dialetto Napoletano*, Home Cooking in Neapolitan Dialect. 〜

Vermicelli co le Pomodoro

Spaghetti with tomatoes

❧ Pick four rotola (a Neapolitan measure of weight, equaling about 33 ounces or 8¼ pounds) of tomatoes. Cut out any blemishes, remove the seeds and water and boil the fruit. When the tomatoes are soft, pass throught a sieve and cook down by a third. When the sauce is sufficiently dense, boil two rotola (four pounds) of vermicelli. Drain the pasta and add it to the sauce along with salt and pepper. Stir and cook the mixture until the sauce has dried and serve.

〜 Tomato sauce was also an important inclusion in the recipe book *La Scienza in Cucina e l'Arte di Mangiar Bene* (Science in Cooking and the Art of Eating Well) by Pellegrino Artusi, published in 1891. The publication of this book was considered the official birth of Italian gastronomy. 〜

Above: Copyright Museo Nazionale delle Paste Alimentari

14

15

70 B.C. b. Virgil, poet

16

17

ZUPPA ALLA PRIMAVERILE

VEGETABLE SOUP

❧ Take some cabbage, carrots, celery, onions, turnips, lettuce, squash, potatoes, beans, and peas. Chop each into very small pieces, wash and drain. Take a saucepan, put in a heaping tablespoon of butter; chop up another small piece of onion and add to butter and fry until onion is golden; then add all the vegetables, salt, and pepper, and cover the saucepan. When the vegetables are half cooked, and their juice has become absorbed, dissolve one tablespoon of tomato paste in one-third of a cup of hot water, and add. Instead of the tomato paste there may be added to the onion, before putting in the vegetables, one tomato, peeled and cut into small pieces. When the tomato is cooked add the vegetables. Then add water, a little at a time, until you have sufficient quantity for two persons. Take a slice of bread and cut into small squares or diamonds—toast or fry as desired—put these into the soup plates, and pour the soup (without straining) over them.

Antonia Isola, Simple Italian Cookery

18

19

ancient Roman festival honoring Mars; weapons are stored away for winter

20

21	
22	
23	
24	
25	
26	
27	

ANTIPASTI

Antipasto means "before the meal." Bartolomeo Scappi, the renowned sixteenth-century chef, popularized antipasti in his tremendous 1570 treatise on food, Opera, and antipasti have since been among Italy's most wonderful dishes.

Lorenza de Medici, Heritage of Italian Cooking

A VISIT TO CREMONA

I did eat fried Frogges in this citie, which is a dish much used in many cities of Italy: they were so curiously dressed, that they did exceedingly delight my palat, the head and the forepart being cut off.

Thomas Coryat, 1608

AMBROSIAL FOOD

The crayfish arrived. There they lay, curled up, juicy, succulent—ambrosial food, delicious! Drowsy with good food and wine, sleepy and content, with reciprocated concord between brain and stomach, we drove back towards Sulmona.

Edward Harvane,
East of Rome: A Journey into the Abruzzi

Opposite: Still life, Giacomo Ceruti. Pinacoteca di Brera, Milano

95

November

28	
29	
30	
31 Halloween	
1 All Saints Day	
2	
3	

APERITIFS
Italian aperitifs come in two varieties—those based on wine (such as Martini), and those based on a spirit (such as Campari). Turin, home of Campari, Carpano, Cinzano, and Martini, is the capital of the aperitif.

World Atlas of Food

THE OLDEST WINE
The oldest red wine in Tuscany is made in the province of Siena and bears the name of Brunello di Montalcino. The first documents about it date back to the 8th century, when the Lombards were masters of the region. This wine must be aged in special wooden barrels for at least four years; otherwise it cannot be bottled as Brunello. One of its exceptional features is that it continues to age indefinitely in the bottle, and its flavour becomes better and more velvety as the years pass. It is made with only one type of grape, the brunello, is produced in limited quantities in a very restricted zone and is bottled by very few producers.

Wilma Pezzini, The Tuscan Cookbook

4

National Unity Day (Italy)

5

6

7

8

9

10

THE PATH TO ROME

In Ronciglione I saw the things that Turner drew; I mean the rocks from which a river springs, and houses all massed together…I ate and drank, asking every one questions of Rome, and I passed under their great gate and pursued the road to the plain.

    Hilaire Belloc

THE VENDEMMIA

Early autumn is the time of the *vendemmia*. Families were out in the vineyards and tubs of grapes were on the move round about the village, occasionally on the backs of donkeys but more often pulled on trailers behind tiny, chuttering tractors. The sharp scent of crushed grapes hung in the alleyways. Piles of grape pressings, brown and acetic, appeared outside the cellars and we peered down into ancient caves where the vats seethed and the barrels stood like totems. Fruit flies, *moscioni*, hung hopefully in the air and met inebriated deaths in one's wine glass.

    Simon Mawer, A Place in Italy,
    set in Avea, an historic village outside Rome

WHEN IN ROME

If in Rome one can readily set oneself to study, then one can do nothing but live. You forget yourself and the world; and to me it is a strange feeling to go about with people who think of nothing but enjoying themselves.

    Lady Hamilton, 1787

Opposite: The Arch of Titus in Rome, G. Healy

COSTUMI POPOLARI LOMBARDI

Milano presso Ant.º Bossi Piazza del Duomo. N.º 4079.

11 *Veterans'/Armistice/Remembrance Day*	### Per fare gnocchi alla Siciliana per dodici persone *To make Sicilian gnocchi for twelve people* ❧ Take a handful of sorrel and one of basil, and a little parsley and chop all this with a knife, then pound it in a mortar together with twelve shelled walnuts. Add four ounces of grated Parmesan, two pounds of dry ricotta, the yolks of six fresh eggs and a handful of dried prunes mixed with four ounces of breadcrumbs, a quarter of an ounce of pepper and quarter of an ounce of cinnamon and three ounces of raisins which have been soaked, and three ounces of shelled pine nuts and very little salt. Have a copper pot handy with plenty of water and salt, put in an onion stuck with cinnamon stick and cloves and let it boil a little. Then remove the onion, and with a spoon dipped in the water take pieces the size of a walnut from the mixture and boil them. Lift them out with a slotted spoon and put them in a dish, pouring over them a pound of melted butter and six ounces of grated Parmesand and one ounce of powdered spicy *mostaccioli* and serve them nice and hot.
12	*Giuseppe Lamma, seventeenth century*
13	**GNOCCHI AND RAVIOLI** 〰 Gnocchi or little dumplings are traditionally made in northern Italy—in Tuscany and in Emilia-Romagna—as well as in Sicily. Another pasta dish of northern Italy is agnolotti, little square ravioli stuffed with meat or spinach, which are native to Piedmont. 〰 World Atlas of Food
14	
15	
16	
17	

18

19

20

21

Festa della Salute, Venice

22

23

24

A REAPER

The first time that I saw you, maiden fair,
Was in a cornfield where you came and reaped:
You'd tucked your skirt up well, and then and there
You set to work, and quick the row you sweeped:
I saw you working, and your way admired;
I saw you fair, and that my love inspired.

Tuscan folk rhyme

December

25	
26	
27	

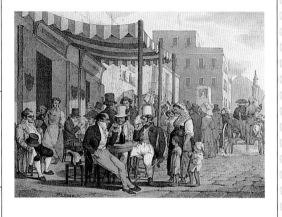

ESPRESSO

Coffee made its way to Italy by way of Turkey, first appearing in Venice, where coffee houses were very popular in the seventeenth century. Espresso, which has the double meaning of "squeezed"—that is, the brew is pressed from the ground coffee—and "fast," first appeared in the early 1900s.

Paul Hoffman, That Fine Italian Hand

28
29
30

1

2

3

4

5

6

7

8

Immaculate Conception (Italy)

65 B.C. b Horace, poet

BOLOGNESE COOKING

The first time I had luncheon at Papagallo [in Bologna], I was comatose for the rest of the day...chickens' breasts cooked in butter and served with thin slices of white truffles, or even richer, layers of turkey and ham oozing with butter, cheese, truffles, and mushrooms, and of the Lambrusco, the dry, sparkling Emilian red wine that seems made by Nature for Bolognese cooking...

H.V. Morton, A Traveller in Italy

THE WHITE TRUFFLE OF PIEDMONT

From Piedmont comes the incredible *tartufo bianco*, or white truffle, a luxurious ingredient that graces many regional dishes. The truffle grows in the clay soil of the area, near hazelnut, oak, and linden trees, and is harvested by dogs.

Lidia Bastianich and Jay Jacobs,
La Cucina di Lidia

Opposite: The Life of Saint Benedict: Monks dining, Luca Signorelli. Monte Oliveto Maggiore

POSTE ITALIANE

35 LIRE

LE OLIVE
(BASILICATA)

.P.S - OFF. CARTE - VALORI - ROMA

C. MEZZANA

Serie "Italia al Lavoro" Anno 1950

9	*Olives Ripening*
	When the olives were ripening at
10	*Christmas in the groves of*
	Bozzano, Igecchia, and
	Massarosa I came home; and
11	*then again at Easter when*
ancient Roman festival honoring all the gods	*Viareggio glowed in the hot*
	Spring sunlight.
	Dante del Fiorentino
12	

13	
14	
	Native to the eastern Mediterranean, olives first appeared in Italy around 400 B.C.— they had been present in Greece for much longer.
15	Hugh Thomas, An Unfinished History of the World

16	**ITALIAN ICES** 〜 Granita, the Italian version of sorbet, originated in southern Italy and in its earliest formulation consisted of citrus juice or coffee mixed with snow. Gelato, or Italian ice cream, first appeared in the seventeenth century. 〜 Lidia Bastianich and Jay Jacobs, La Cucina di Lidia
17	
18	
19 ancient Roman festival honoring Saturn, god of seed-corn	*Fellowship* *I could not understand his songs nor he mine, but there was wine in common between us, and salami and a merry heart, bread which is like the bond of all mankind...* Hilaire Belloc, The Path to Rome
20	
21	**REASONS TO DRINK** It is well to remember that there are five reasons for drinking: the arrival of a friend; one's present or future thirst; the excellence of the wine; or any other reason. *Old Latin saying*
22 solstice	

23	
24	
25 Christmas	
26	
27	
28	
29	

PANETTONE

Panettone, a spiced and fruited bread, has become synonymous with Christmas in Italy. The legend of panettone is that it was made by a Milanese baker named Tony (panettone means "Tony's bread") for his beloved. The bread was so good that everyone wanted some.

World Atlas of Food

Torta detta marzapane

Marzipan cake

The cake known as "marzipan" is made as follows. For a night and a day leave in cold water some almonds which have been peeled with as much care as possible. Then pound them, continuing to add a little water so they will not give out oil. If you wish the cake to turn out excellent, add an amount of sugar equal to the almonds. When you have pounded everything well, dilute it with rosewater, and put it into a pan lined with a thin sheet of pastry, moistening again with rosewater, and then put it in the oven and once more moisten it continually with rosewater so it will not become too dry. It may be cooked over the fire if you follow the cooking with care so that the cake does not end up burnt rather than cooked. This cake must be flat, not too thick, if it is to be good. I do not recall ever having eaten anything more delicious with my friend Patizio the elder. Indeed, it is very nourishing, quite digestible, is good for the chest, the kidneys and the liver, and it makes the sperm grow, stimulates one to the pleasures of Venus, and refreshes the urine.

Bartolomeo Platina, De Honesta Voluptate ac Valetudine (Concerning Honest Pleasure and Well-being), fifteenth century

La Vigilia, the traditional Italian Christmas Eve meal, is usually based on seafood dishes—as Christmas Eve is a day of abstinence from meat. In Rome, for example, the classic dish is capitone, or fattened eel.

Lidia Bastianich and Jay Jacobs, La Cucina di Lidia

January

30

31

1

New Year's Day

2

3

4

5

Gelato di Mandorla

Milk of Almond Ice

❧ Take one-half pound of almonds. Remove the shells and skins, and put them into a large receptacle of cold water. Add three bitter almonds to the number. Remove them from the water, and pound them up in a bowl, adding from time to time a little water. Then add more water and put them into a cheese-cloth and wring it, to extract all the juices you can. Then pound them some more, adding water, and squeeze out as before. To the milk you have extracted from the almonds add four tablespoons of powdered sugar and one-half tablespoon of orange water; put into the freezer and freeze. If desired, you can put half the quantity of almonds and the other half of cantaloupe seeds, pound together, and proceed in the same manner. This combination is refreshing and delicious.

Antonia Isola, Simple Italian Cookery

1995

JANUARY

M	T	W	T	F	S	S
						1
2	3	4	5	6	7	8
9	10	11	12	13	14	15
16	17	18	19	20	21	22
23	24	25	26	27	28	29
30	31					

FEBRUARY

M	T	W	T	F	S	S
		1	2	3	4	5
6	7	8	9	10	11	12
13	14	15	16	17	18	19
20	21	22	23	24	25	26
27	28					

MARCH

M	T	W	T	F	S	S
		1	2	3	4	5
6	7	8	9	10	11	12
13	14	15	16	17	18	19
20	21	22	23	24	25	26
27	28	29	30	31		

APRIL

M	T	W	T	F	S	S
					1	2
3	4	5	6	7	8	9
10	11	12	13	14	15	16
17	18	19	20	21	22	23
24	25	26	27	28	29	30

MAY

M	T	W	T	F	S	S
1	2	3	4	5	6	7
8	9	10	11	12	13	14
15	16	17	18	19	20	21
22	23	24	25	26	27	28
29	30	31				

JUNE

M	T	W	T	F	S	S
			1	2	3	4
5	6	7	8	9	10	11
12	13	14	15	16	17	18
19	20	21	22	23	24	25
26	27	28	29	30		

JULY

M	T	W	T	F	S	S
					1	2
3	4	5	6	7	8	9
10	11	12	13	14	15	16
17	18	19	20	21	22	23
24	25	26	27	28	29	30
31						

AUGUST

M	T	W	T	F	S	S
	1	2	3	4	5	6
7	8	9	10	11	12	13
14	15	16	17	18	19	20
21	22	23	24	25	26	27
28	29	30	31			

SEPTEMBER

M	T	W	T	F	S	S
				1	2	3
4	5	6	7	8	9	10
11	12	13	14	15	16	17
18	19	20	21	22	23	24
25	26	27	28	29	30	

OCTOBER

M	T	W	T	F	S	S
						1
2	3	4	5	6	7	8
9	10	11	12	13	14	15
16	17	18	19	20	21	22
23	24	25	26	27	28	29
30	31					

NOVEMBER

M	T	W	T	F	S	S
	1	2	3	4	5	
6	7	8	9	10	11	12
13	14	15	16	17	18	19
20	21	22	23	24	25	26
27	28	29	30			

DECEMBER

M	T	W	T	F	S	S
				1	2	3
4	5	6	7	8	9	10
11	12	13	14	15	16	17
18	19	20	21	22	23	24
25	26	27	28	29	30	31

1996

JANUARY
M	T	W	T	F	S	S
1	2	3	4	5	6	7
8	9	10	11	12	13	14
15	16	17	18	19	20	21
22	23	24	25	26	27	28
29	30	31				

FEBRUARY
M	T	W	T	F	S	S
			1	2	3	4
5	6	7	8	9	10	11
12	13	14	15	16	17	18
19	20	21	22	23	24	25
26	27	28	29			

MARCH
M	T	W	T	F	S	S
				1	2	3
4	5	6	7	8	9	10
11	12	13	14	15	16	17
18	19	20	21	22	23	24
25	26	27	28	29	30	31

APRIL
M	T	W	T	F	S	S
1	2	3	4	5	6	7
8	9	10	11	12	13	14
15	16	17	18	19	20	21
22	23	24	25	26	27	28
29	30					

MAY
M	T	W	T	F	S	S
		1	2	3	4	5
6	7	8	9	10	11	12
13	14	15	16	17	18	19
20	21	22	23	24	25	26
27	28	29	30	31		

JUNE
M	T	W	T	F	S	S
					1	2
3	4	5	6	7	8	9
10	11	12	13	14	15	16
17	18	19	20	21	22	23
24	25	26	27	28	29	30

JULY
M	T	W	T	F	S	S
1	2	3	4	5	6	7
8	9	10	11	12	13	14
15	16	17	18	19	20	21
22	23	24	25	26	27	28
29	30	31				

MARCA DEPOSITATA

AUGUST
M	T	W	T	F	S	S
			1	2	3	4
5	6	7	8	9	10	11
12	13	14	15	16	17	18
19	20	21	22	23	24	25
26	27	28	29	30	31	

SEPTEMBER
M	T	W	T	F	S	S
						1
2	3	4	5	6	7	8
9	10	11	12	13	14	15
16	17	18	19	20	21	22
23	24	25	26	27	28	29
30						

OCTOBER
M	T	W	T	F	S	S
	1	2	3	4	5	6
7	8	9	10	11	12	13
14	15	16	17	18	19	20
21	22	23	24	25	26	27
28	29	30	31			

NOVEMBER
M	T	W	T	F	S	S
				1	2	3
4	5	6	7	8	9	10
11	12	13	14	15	16	17
18	19	20	21	22	23	24
25	26	27	28	29	30	

DECEMBER
M	T	W	T	F	S	S
						1
2	3	4	5	6	7	8
9	10	11	12	13	14	15
16	17	18	19	20	21	22
23	24	25	26	27	28	29
30	31					

1997

JANUARY
M	T	W	T	F	S	S
		1	2	3	4	5
6	7	8	9	10	11	12
13	14	15	16	17	18	19
20	21	22	23	24	25	26
27	28	29	30	31		

FEBRUARY
M	T	W	T	F	S	S
					1	2
3	4	5	6	7	8	9
10	11	12	13	14	15	16
17	18	19	20	21	22	23
24	25	26	27	28		

MARCH
M	T	W	T	F	S	S
					1	2
3	4	5	6	7	8	9
10	11	12	13	14	15	16
17	18	19	20	21	22	23
24	25	26	27	28	29	30
31						

APRIL
M	T	W	T	F	S	S
	1	2	3	4	5	6
7	8	9	10	11	12	13
14	15	16	17	18	19	20
21	22	23	24	25	26	27
28	29	30				

MAY
M	T	W	T	F	S	S
			1	2	3	4
5	6	7	8	9	10	11
12	13	14	15	16	17	18
19	20	21	22	23	24	25
26	27	28	29	30	31	

JUNE
M	T	W	T	F	S	S
						1
2	3	4	5	6	7	8
9	10	11	12	13	14	15
16	17	18	19	20	21	22
23	24	25	26	27	28	29
30						

JULY
M	T	W	T	F	S	S
	1	2	3	4	5	6
7	8	9	10	11	12	13
14	15	16	17	18	19	20
21	22	23	24	25	26	27
28	29	30	31			

AUGUST
M	T	W	T	F	S	S
				1	2	3
4	5	6	7	8	9	10
11	12	13	14	15	16	17
18	19	20	21	22	23	24
25	26	27	28	29	30	31

SEPTEMBER
M	T	W	T	F	S	S
1	2	3	4	5	6	7
8	9	10	11	12	13	14
15	16	17	18	19	20	21
22	23	24	25	26	27	28
29	30					

OCTOBER
M	T	W	T	F	S	S
	1	2	3	4	5	
6	7	8	9	10	11	12
13	14	15	16	17	18	19
20	21	22	23	24	25	26
27	28	29	30	31		

NOVEMBER
M	T	W	T	F	S	S
					1	2
3	4	5	6	7	8	9
10	11	12	13	14	15	16
17	18	19	20	21	22	23
24	25	26	27	28	29	30

DECEMBER
M	T	W	T	F	S	S
1	2	3	4	5	6	7
8	9	10	11	12	13	14
15	16	17	18	19	20	21
22	23	24	25	26	27	28
29	30	31				

Acknowledgments

The editors and publishers would like to thank the following for their invaluable help with the preparation of this book: Jan Hughes, Julia Cain, Kathy Warinner, Carla Bertini, Paddy Macdonald, and Giuseppe Agoccioni.

The following gave permission for material to be used:

Olive Tree

PICTURES
AFE/CPS: Caramelle Venchi advertisement (19); *Roma: Trattoria popolare. Stampa ottocentesca* (43); Amaro Ramazzotti advertisement (110)

By courtesy of Agnesi: advertisements (16, 79)

By courtesy of Barilla America, Inc., Norwalk, CT: pasta-making implements (20, 42, 59, 62, 95, 106, 116); pasta charts (16, 17, 58, 101); advertisements (15, 17, 33, 34, 65 top, 66, 67, 101, 116, 117, 118)

From the archives of Bertolli USA, Inc, Secaucus, NJ: Bertolli toothpick holder circa 1950 (28); Bertolli olive oil print ad circa 1965 (109)

By courtesy of Carlo Alberto Bertozzi, Management Resources of America, Norwalk, CT: *Parmegiano-Reggiano Bertozzi Parma*, A.L. Mauzan, 1930 (back cover, 11)

Bettmann Archive: undated engraving (7); *Course of the Empire: Savage State (Rome)*, Thomas Cole (38); Venice. Panorama of S. Giorgio, The Doge's Palace, and two gondoliers (46); Venice. View of gondoliers on the Grand Canal near the Cavalli Palace, with the church S. Salute in the background (47); Villa of Stabia, harbor of Pompeii, fresco from a Stabian house (74); A baker shop, detail of a fresco from Pompeii (75); *The Arch of Titus in Rome*, G. Healy (98); *Still life with grapes, peaches and pears*, Frans Snyders (106)

By courtesy of Cinzano International; advertisements (96, 97, 105)

By courtesy of Cirio: advertisements (72, 92)

Copyright The Gifted Line, John Grossman, Inc.,

Point Richmond, CA: Lucca Olive Oil tin, 1906 (28); champagne bucket, c. 1890–1900 (114); Fernet-Branca Bitter, c. 1895 (115)

Giraudon/Art Resource, NY: illumination from *Tacuinum Sanitatis de Sex Rebus*, Ibn Botlan (22)

By courtesy of Illy Caffè: advertisement (41)

Erich Lessing/Art Resource: *The Marriage at Cana*, Paolo Veronese (37); *Autumn*, Giuseppe Archimboldo (87)

Lyons Ltd. Antique Prints: map of southern Italy (endpapers); engravings (12, 13); fruit (20, 56, 71, 79, 113, 118); garlic (23, 120); olives (28, 109, 119), cheeses (10, 33, 118); vineyard (48, 116); tower of Pisa (49, 117); fish (69); *Wine Making at Pola, in Istria* (76); marketplace (78)

Copyright Museo Nazionale delle Paste Alimentari: front cover image; (29); (84); (91 top)

Nimatallah/Art Resource, NY: *Figs*, Bartolomeo Bimbi (57)

Northwind Picture Archives: *The Oysterman* (69); two kitchen interiors (95)

By courtesy of Pastificio di Nola: Pasta "Raffaele" advertisement (85)

Poste Italiane-Museo Storico P.T. Roma: *Bozzetto per il Francobollo "Prima giornata mondiale per l'Alimentazione,"* Giorgio Sciltian (71, 110); *Raccolta delle olive,* Corrado Mezzana (108)

Quantity Postcards: (90)

H. Armstrong Roberts: *The Summer,* Giuseppe Archimboldo (54)

By courtesy of San Francisco Public Library: (86, 104)

Scala/Art Resource, New York: *Apollo, Bacco e Sileno al convito nuziale,* Giulio Romano (6); *Pianta panoramica di Genova,* Danti Ignazio (8); *Piatto a pesce campano* (9, 103); *Veduta di Genova nel 1481* (9); *La Cuoca,* Bernardo Strozzi (14); *Banchetto,* Marcello Fogolino (21); *Vertumnus,* Giuseppe Archimboldo (24); *Canestro di frutta,* Caravaggio (25); *La Cucina,* Vincenzo Campi (26-27); *Venditore di formaggio,* Giuseppe Maria Mitelli (32); *Carta del Mediterraneo* (39); *Still life II,* Jacopo da Empoli (45); four illuminations from *Codici "Officium Beatae Virginis"*: *giugno, la miet itura* (51), *iuglio, la batt itura* (63), *settembre, la vendemmia* (5, 77), *ottobre, la raccolta delle rape* (89); *Market scene,* fresco, late 15th century (53); *Natura morta con frutta,* Vincenzo Campi (60); *Cooking.* Detail of lunette, Federigo Zuccaro (68); *Still life with cherries,* Bartolomeo Bimbi (73); *Piatto di baccelli,* Giovanna Garzoni (80); *Mangiatore di fagioli,* Annibale Carracci (81); *Storie di S. Barbara,* Lorenzo Lotto (82-83); *Still Life,* Giacomo Ceruti (94); *The Life of Saint Benedict,* Luca Signorelli (107)

By courtesy of Sorelle Nurzia by Selezione Totalia, Bologna: advertisement (30)

Studio Pizzi: Menu del Piroscafo (frontispiece); Cioccolato Perugina advertisement (18); Bitter Campari advertisement (40); *Taverna Napoletana* (61); *Vendita e mangia maccheroni* (64); Vini Spumanti Gancia advertisement (70); Cirio advertisement (93); *Costumi Popolari Lombardi* (100); Pastificio Italiano Torino (102); *Bottega del caffè al molo* (65, 104); Liquore Strega advertisement (111); dal 1395 a.D. Panettone di Milano, G. Cova & C. (112)

TEXT

Doubleday a division of Bantam, Doubleday, Dell Publishing Group, Inc.: from *La Cucina di Lidia,* by Lidia Bastianich and Jay Jacobs, copyright 1990, recipes for Straciatella and Scarola (55)

Italian Trade Commission: from *Columbus Menu,* by Stefano Milioni, copyright 1992, recipes for Salsa di Pomodoro (90), Pomodori alla Certosina (91), and Vermicelli co le Pomodoro (91)

Italy, Italy: from the March/April 1994 issue of *Italy, Italy,* recipes for Pasta alla Norma (16), Fettucine alla Papalina (17), and Pastiera (36)

Peter Owen Publishers: from *The Complete Poems of Michelangelo,* translated by Joseph Tusiani, lines from 3 poems (19, 25)

Random House UK: from *The Heritage of Italian Cooking* by Lorenza de' Medici, copyright 1990, translations of ancient Italian recipes (52, 65, 74, 88, 101, 113)

In an anthology such as this it is not always possible to acknowledge or even find the copyright holders of certain material. The publishers have made every effort, but apologize in advance for any lapse. They would be pleased to hear from anyone who has not been acknowledged.

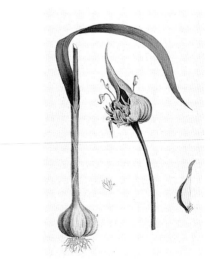

Fiorenzo

Calvi

P. Padura
C. Gordona
Morsetto
C. Fuschiaro
Gulf of Preto
Berettale

L. Bolsena

Viterbo

Cometo

STATES

Seago
C. Pellegrino
S. Andrea

Gulf of Sagona
Giresliesa
Jessore

Civita Vecchia

ROME

Tivoli

C. Ferro
Ajaccio

Ogana

Vialmero

R. Tiber

Albano

Gulf of Ajaccio

Valenza

Nettno

C. Muro
Vico

C. Santiero
T.A Ciprian

C. & Mt Circe

C. Canales I.

G. of Venaro
S.ta Maria

STRAIT   OF   BONIFACIO

BONIFACIO

Astinara I.
Sevenmenica

Reparata
Maddalena I.
Caprera I.

C. Falcone
G. of Asinara
Sassari

Aragonese
Terranova
Tavolara I.
Molari I.

Sassari

CAPO D E L Posada
C. Comino

SASSARI

Oristano
SARDINIA
Terralba
C. Monte-Santo

Bosa

C. Bellavista

G. of Oristano
CAPO   CAGLIARI

Villacidro
Chirra I.

Iglesias

Cagliari

C. Forato

Massarosa
Quartu

Serpentaria I.

Villarey

Antisco
C. Carbonara

G. of Palmas

BENEVENTO

NAPLES AND VESUVIUS

SCALE

Miles

C. Vito
C. S.ta

Maritimo
Levanzo
Trapani

Favignana

C. Roso
Marsala

S